MEDIA CENTER

D0575803

I Could

Esther Morris

MIDTOWN SCHOOL
MEDIA CENTER

11222133044

Do That!
Gets Women the Vote

Linda Arms White
Pictures by Nancy Carpenter

MELANIE KROUPA BOOKS

FARRAR STRAUS GIROUX ◆ NEW YORK

To my childhood days in Wyoming, the Equality State, which taught me, like Esther,

"I could do that"

and to Nancy Phillips, whose CAN DO attitude is a daily inspiration

—L.A.W.

To Hillary

—N.C.

Text copyright © 2005 by Linda Arms White
Illustrations copyright © 2005 by Nancy Carpenter
All rights reserved
Distributed in Canada by Douglas & McIntyre Publishing Group
Color separations by Chroma Graphics PTE Ltd.
Printed and bound in China by South China Printing Co. Ltd.
Designed by Robbin Gourley
First edition, 2005
3   5   7   9   10   8   6   4   2

www.fsgkidsbooks.com

Library of Congress Cataloging-in-Publication Data

White, Linda Arms.
    I could do that : Esther Morris gets women the vote / by Linda Arms White ; pictures
by Nancy Carpenter.— 1st ed.
        p. cm.
    Summary: In 1869, a woman whose "can-do" attitude had shaped her life was instrumental
in making Wyoming the first territory to allow women to vote, then became the first woman
to hold public office in the United States.
    ISBN-13: 978-0-374-33527-4
    ISBN-10: 0-374-33527-3
    1. Morris, Esther Hobart, 1814–1902—Juvenile literature.   2. Suffragists—Wyoming—
Biography—Juvenile literature.   3. Women—Suffrage—Wyoming—History—19th century—
Juvenile literature.   [1. Morris, Esther Hobart, 1814–1902.   2. Suffragists.   3. Justices of the
peace.   4. Women—Biography.]   I. Carpenter, Nancy, ill.   II. Title.

JK1899.M67M55 2005
324.6′23′092—dc21
[B]
                                                                                                                2003051417

In 1820, six-year-old Esther McQuigg studied her mother making tea. "I could do that," she said.

"Make tea?" asked Mama. "The older girls do that."

"But I want to learn," said Esther, and she did. She pumped water into the kettle and set it on the woodstove to boil. She scooped tea leaves into the teapot, then poured steaming water over them. Esther strained the tea into cups, one for her mother, one for herself.

As they sat near the window of their New York house, Esther saw men riding by in their best suits, some carrying flags.

"Where are those men going, Mama?" asked Esther.

"They are going to vote for the next president of the United States," Mama said.

"Will Papa vote?"

"Yes, Papa always votes."

"Will you vote, Mama?"

"No, dear, only men can vote."

When Esther was eight, she watched her mother sew a fine seam. The needle pulled thread in and out, in and out, tracking tiny, even stitches across the fabric. Esther felt her hands mimicking her mother's. "I could do that," she said. And she did.

She made clothes for her doll from scraps, and when her stitches became neat and straight, she sewed a shirt for Papa.

When Esther was eleven, her mother died, and for the first time she saw her father cry. He gathered his eleven children together. "I don't know what we'll do without your mama," he said. "I'm depending on each of you to be brave and to take care of one another."

Esther, eighth of the eleven, cried, too. But then she said, "I can do that, Papa." And she did.

When Esther was nineteen, six feet tall, and on her own, she earned a living making dresses with leg-of-mutton sleeves for society ladies.

When the ladies wanted hats to match the dresses, Esther designed and made those, too. Soon, she thought of opening a millinery shop.

"You are much too young to run a business," she was told.

"I don't see why" was Esther's reply, and with that, she opened a hat shop in Owego, New York.

Esther started attending abolitionist meetings at her church. But a throng of people who believed in the right to own slaves threatened to stop the meetings even if they had to tear down the Baptist church where they were held.

"You can't do that," Esther said. "I'll stop anyone who tries."

When Esther was twenty-eight, she married Artemus Slack and, a few years later, had a son they called Archy.

But when Artemus died in an accident, Esther made a big decision. "I'm moving to Illinois," she told her friends. "I'll claim the land Artemus owned there and raise our son."

"You can't do that!" her friends cried. "Illinois is the very edge of civilization. It's full of dangerous people and wild animals."

"Yes," she said, "I can." And that was that.

In Illinois, she fought long and hard to claim Artemus's land, but was denied her inheritance because she was female. So Esther opened another hat shop.

Esther met and married John Morris, a merchant and immigrant from Poland, and in 1851 she gave birth to twin boys, Edward and Robert.

But John had a hard time making a living. So while Esther raised the children, cooked the meals, and washed the clothes, she helped earn the money, too.

When Esther was forty-six, she went with John to the presidential election polls and watched through the window while he voted.

"You know," she told him when he came out, "I could do that."

"Politics is the business of men, my dear," he said.

"Humph," said Esther. "It's our country, too."

When war broke out between the Northern
and Southern states, Esther was proud that Archy joined
the victorious fight of the North to end slavery. Soon after, an amendment to
the Constitution granted Negro men all rights of citizenship, including the
right to vote.

When Esther heard Susan B. Anthony speaking out about woman's rights,
Esther began to hope that someday women might vote, too.

In 1869, when Esther was fifty-five, she and her eighteen-year-old sons moved to the newly formed Wyoming Territory, where John and Archy, who'd gone there the year before, waited.

Esther and the boys traveled by train across miles of prairie, then by stage over rocky hills to South Pass City, a dusty, hurriedly built town where gold had been found. Most of the two thousand people who lived there were rowdy young men. They worked in the mines by day, drank in the saloons by night.

The Morrises moved their belongings into a small log cabin, and South Pass City became home. John ran a saloon.

Archy bought a printing press and started a newspaper.

Esther opened another hat shop.

But with six men to every woman, there was always a need for someone to nurse the sick and wounded, sew clothes, help deliver babies, and give motherly advice to the few young women in town. "I could do that," Esther said.

And she did.

One day, Esther read a proclamation tacked to a wall: **ALL MALE CITIZENS 21 AND OLDER ARE CALLED TO VOTE IN THE FIRST TERRITORIAL ELECTIONS.** Esther looked around at the disorderly young men.

"It's time I did that," she said.

When Esther's sons watched her march toward home, they knew it was more likely that things were about to change than that things would stay the same.

Esther invited the two men running for the territorial legislature to her house to speak to the citizens. Then she sent out invitations to the most influential people in the territory: "Come for tea, and talk to the candidates."

She scrubbed her tiny home from top to bottom, washed the curtains, and ironed her best dress.

When the candidates and guests arrived, Esther served them tea.
"One thing I like about Wyoming," she said, "is how everyone is
important. It takes all of us to run the town, women as well as men."
"Yes," her guests agreed.
"And it's a place where people aren't afraid to try new things."
Her guests agreed again.

Esther smiled. She turned to the candidates. "Then, would you, if elected, introduce a bill in the legislature that would allow women to vote?"

Suddenly, in that tiny room full of people, not a sound was heard.

Finally, Colonel William Bright spoke. "Mrs. Morris, my wife would like to vote, too. She is intelligent and well educated. Truth be told, she would be a more informed voter than I. If I am elected, I will introduce that bill."

Not wanting to be outdone, the other candidate, Herman Nickerson, also agreed.

Applause broke out in that tiny cabin, and Esther dropped to her chair. "Thank you," she said.

People warned her that once the bill was introduced, the men of the legislature would have to approve it. And the governor would have to sign it. This had never happened anywhere. Why did she think it could happen here?

But Esther had seen that things that were not likely to happen, happened every day. She wrote letters and visited legislators to make sure this bill would happen, too.

And it did. On December 10, 1869, Governor John Campbell signed this bill into law!

WYOMING WOMEN

GET THE VOTE!

Women across the country rejoiced for the women of Wyoming.

But some people didn't like it. Only eight days later, Judge James Stillman, the county's justice of the peace, turned in his resignation. He refused to administer justice in a place where women helped make the laws.

Word went out that a new justice of the peace was needed.

Esther's boys turned to her. "Mama, *you* could do that," they said. And so she applied.

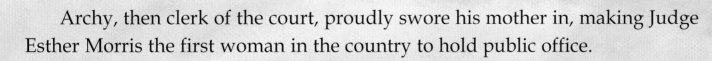

Archy, then clerk of the court, proudly swore his mother in, making Judge Esther Morris the first woman in the country to hold public office.

But Judge Stillman refused to turn over the official court docket to Esther.

"Never mind," she said. "Archy, will you please go to the Mercantile and buy me a ledger? I'll start my own docket."

And, of course, she did.

On September 6, 1870, one year after her tea party, Judge Esther Morris put on her best dress and walked with her husband, John, and her sons down the dusty street to the polling place. She would be one of a thousand Wyoming women voting that day, the first ever given that right permanently by any governing body in the United States.

As they walked, John, who still didn't think women should vote, tried to coach her on which candidates and issues to vote for.

Esther held up her hand.

"I can do this," she said.

And she did.

Author's Note

Only the barest facts from church, cemetery, and public records are known about Esther Morris's early life, her millinery business, and her two marriages. Esther's church in Owego was the first antislavery church established in the country. Her interest in equal rights extended to woman's suffrage, as recorded in letters to her cousin. It is said that in 1895, Esther attended the National Suffrage Convention as an elected delegate.

While many historians believe that the story of her tea party is true, as Captain H. G. Nickerson, one of the candidates, reported some years later, others question whether it really happened. All, however, agree that Esther was instrumental in gaining woman's suffrage in Wyoming Territory. They also agree that when her son swore her in as justice of the peace in South Pass City, she became the first female judge and the first woman in the United States to hold a political office.

In spite of all her "firsts," Esther never voted for president. It wasn't until 1920, fifty-one years after Esther's Wyoming tea party and eighteen years after her death, that the Nineteenth Amendment to the Constitution granted all women across the United States the right to vote in national elections.

Esther's likeness stands in front of the Wyoming State Capitol and in the National Statuary Hall Collection in the United States Capitol.

Today, women throughout much of the world vote, hold office, and take an active role in their country's government. However, there are still some countries where women's voices are not heard. If Esther were there, she would get out her teapot and get to work.

Resources

BOOKS AND ARTICLES

Acceptance of the Statue of Esther Morris, Presented by the State of Wyoming. Washington, D.C.: United States Government Printing Office, 1961.

Cheney, Lynne. "It All Started in Wyoming." *American Heritage Magazine*, April 1978.

Dobler, Lavinia. *Esther Morris: First Woman Justice of the Peace*. Riverton, Wyo.: Big Bend Press, 1993.

Larson, T. A. *History of Wyoming*. Lincoln, Neb.: University of Nebraska Press, 1965.

Massie, Michael A. "The Roots of Woman Suffrage in Wyoming." *Annals of Wyoming*, Spring 1990.

Sherlock, James L. *South Pass and Its Tales*. Basin, Wyo.: Wolverine Gallery, 1978.

WEB SITES

Esther Morris

http://www.aoc.gov/cc/art/nsh/Morris.htm

http://lcweb2.loc.gov/ammem/today/dec10.html

South Pass City

http://wyoparks.state.wy.us/south.htm

Woman Suffrage

http://www.suffragist.com/timeline.htm

VISIT

South Pass City State Historical Site, South Pass, Wyoming

Esther Morris brewed a pot of tea that heated up the woman's suffrage movement and won the vote for the women of Wyoming Territory in 1869. Gradually, more territories and states gave women the vote:

1896
Idaho

1912
Kansas

1912
Oregon

1914
Montana

1914
Nevada

1917
Arkansas
(Presidential
election only)

1917
Rhode Island
(Presidential
election only)

1918
Michigan

1918
Oklahoma

1919
Indiana
(Presidential
election only)

1919
Iowa
(Presidential
election only)

1919
Maine
(Presidential
election only)

1919
Ohio
(Presidential
election only)

1919
Tennessee
(Presidential
election only)

1919
Wisconsin
(Presidential
election only)

FREETOWN ELEMENTARY SCHOOL
11222133044   92 MORRIS
I could do that! : Esther